Download the UNOFFICIAL Hip-Hop Sticker Book FREE!

Get the **UNOFFICIAL Hip-Hop Sticker Book FREE!**

I am only looking for your email. You will receive emails with updates on new releases, exclusive images, original audio, and be eligible for free advance copies of series books. **You can opt out at any time.**

http://eepurl.com/cku-12

BEHIND THE MUSIC TALES BOOKS

N.W.A: The Aftermath

The Real Eminem: Broke City Trash Rapper

The Real Destiny's Child:: The Writing's On The Wall

New York State of Mind 1.0

The Reasonings of Buju Banton, Bounty Killer & Sizzla

Magnolia Home of tha Soliders: Behind the Scenes with the Cash Money Millionaires)

The Real 213

The Real MC Eiht: Geah

The Real Diddy

The Real Daft Punk

BEHINDTHEMUSICTALES.COM

Praise for Harris Rosen

This guy! I plead the fifth. This guy is nuts."
- Eminem

"Dope questions, man. Very insightful, very thoughtful."
- Guru (Gang Starr)

"You like a Psychiatrist or some shit? This shit is just coming out but go ahead."
- Mary J. Blige

"Definitely a real interview! Digging deep up in there, man. Not afraid to ask questions!"
- K-Ci Hailey (Jodeci)

"The Wizard asked me for a copy of your magazine."
- Guy-Manuel de Homem-Christo (Daft Punk)

"You didn't wear your glasses, and you haven't carried your hearing aid. What else is wrong with you?"
- Bushwick Bill

"Peace and blessing, Brother Harris. Thank you for inspiring my words. Keep 'yo balance."
- Erykah Badu

"Can I see that pen?"
- Bobby Brown

"What else do you want to know? Talk to me."
- Aaliyah

Behind The Music Tales 7.0

New York State of Mind 1.0

1992 - 1993

Exclusive Interviews with
Tragedy Khadafi, Brand Nubian,
Pete Rock & C.L. Smooth

By Harris Rosen

Art by Folly Art

Behind The Music Tales

Copyright

© 2016 by Peace! Carving and Harris Rosen.

All rights reserved under International and Pan American Copyright Conventions. The Author has provided this e-book for your personal use only. It may not be resold or transferred to others. You may not make this e-book publicly available in any way. No part of this e-book may be reproduced or transmitted in any form by any means, electronic, mechanical, scanned, recording, or distributed in any printed, or audio form without written permission.

Published by Peace! Carving

First edition November 2016

ISBN: 978-0-9812587-7-5 (Print)

ISBN: 978-0-9812587-8-2 (Digital)

Mr. Heller Press

Heller HQ

QB

Spadina-Fort York

Toronto, ON

M5V 2B3 Canada

Dedication

This series is dedicated to my son Louis, late father, mother, sister, grandmother & the late Raymond Wallace.

Thank you for a lifetime of support and encouragement. I would not be here without you.

Acknowledgments

I wish to personally thank the following people for their contributions to my inspiration and knowledge and other help in creating this book: Salman "Ylook" Rana, Ice, J. Alexander Ferron, Dru Silver, Arty, Folly, Mark Reed, Rob Harris, Peter Cherniawski, Joey DAMMIT! Ian Steaman, Eon Sinclair, Jr., Todd DeKoker, Phil Demetro, James Watt, Chandler Bolt, William J. Genereux, Peter Lazanik, Rishi Persaud.

Contents

Preface 1

Chapter 1: Tragedy Khadafi 6

In The Beginning 9

The Streets 13

The Message 17

Bullet 20

Plans 24

Next 28

Album Discography 30

Music Videos 32

Chapter 2: Brand Nubian 33

Punks Jump Up To Get Beat Down 35

Business 38

Grand Puba 40

Faith 42

Revolution 52

Knowledge Is Power 57

Next 60

Album Discography 63

Music Videos 65

Chapter 3: Pete Rock & C.L. Smooth 68

In The Beginning.. 70

The Process 71

The Message 74

Ghost 76

Nobody Beats The Biz 79

Future 81

Next 83

Album Discography... 85

Music Videos 87

Who Is Harris Rosen? 90

Other Books By Harris Rosen 92

Preface

There will be several New York State of Mind volumes within the **Behind the Music Tales** series.

New York City is the birthplace of Hip-Hop, ground zero. Its sons and daughters are forever claiming a leg up on those dedicated to the Art Form of any other part of the world. Key artists, personalities and phenomenon walk its streets on the day. The Five Boroughs and then some live and breathe Hip-Hop. It's a way of life and a birthright.

New York State of Mind 1.0 feature 1992 and 1993 in-person interviews with Intelligent Hoodlum, Brand Nubian, and Pete Rock & C.L. Smooth. Each was instrumental in and furthered Hip-Hop in their unique manner. The title pays homage to the Nas song "N.Y. State of Mind" of his classic 1994 album, **Illmatic**, produced by DJ Premier straight out of the dungeons of rap. The song itself pays tribute to "Streets of New York." The vivid Kool G. Rap & DJ Polo track that led off their 1990 album **Wanted Dead or Alive**. Not to be confused with Billy Joel's fan favourite, "New York State of Mind," dating back to 1976.

The 80s developed and presented a parade of money earning Hip-Hop artists that eclipsed the highest of projected sales figures. What had once consisted of a savvy cadre of astute forward-thinking independents spread to the corporate world of the major labels.

On the heels of the groundbreaking RUN-D.M.C. and Aerosmith single "Walk This Way," and the Beastie Boys stream of singles leading up to "(You Gotta Fight For Your Right (To Party".

Gone were the days that one could own or be in the know about almost every Hip-Hop crew. The Art Form was omnipresent as major labels began to snap up buzzing and bubbling independent labels, artists and groups with their ears to the streets. Diversity, quality, innovation and influence ruled the day. The Golden Age of Hip-Hop was in full effect, and Eric B. became President for real.

During this period a movement of conscious Rappers captured the ears and eyes of a nation of millions picking up where groups like Public Enemy and filmmakers such as Spike Lee had left off.

A&M Records, the home of Bryan Adams, Sting and Supertramp was in on the action with the release of the **Intelligent Hoodlum** album on June 19, 1990. Known as the kid who came up under the wings of super-producer Marley Marl and the legendary Juice Crew, Intelligent Hoodlum arrived on the scene with fluid flow and a powerful conscious message riding the beats of Marley Marl and Large Professor of Main Source.

A&M Records moved Intelligent Hoodlum over to its very own fresh imprint, Tuff Break, which released **Tragedy: Saga of a Hoodlum** on June 22, 1993. In the summer of 1993, Tragedy Khadafi travelled to Toronto with Tuff Break head honcho Evan Forster to promote the album.

The featured interview took place at the first Peace! HQ with the assistance of Ice. Tragedy spoke on his early days on the streets, Marley Marl, prison, the album, corporate America, religion, and his plans for the future.

Brand Nubian, composed of Grand Puba, Derek X, Lord Jamar and DJ Alamo, signed with Elektra Records in 1989 and released their self-titled single laced with smooth conscious rhymes over the funk backbeats of Parliament and Cameo on May 22, 1989. When their debut album, **All For One** was issued on December 4, 1990, it entered the realm of classics where it lives to this day. Unfortunately, Grand Puba mysteriously parted way with the group at the tail end of 1991 and began a solo career taking DJ Alamo with him. Derek X, now Sadat X, and Lord Jamar recruited DJ Sincere and came back hard, and heavy on January 12, 1993, with the "Punks Jump Up To Get Beat Down" single. The **In God We Trust** album followed on February 2, 1993.

The featured interview with Lord Jamar, Sadat X and DJ Sincere took place over lunch inside downtown Toronto's Jerk Pit shortly after the release of **In God We Trust**, with the assistance of Dru Silver and Ice. It made for a relaxing atmosphere and orders for fruit punch and snapper can be heard on the recording. Brand Nubian was chill and open to speak on any subject. Lord Jamar, Sadat X and DJ Sincere spoke candidly on a variety of topics relating to the group. Their personal spiritual beliefs, the bootleg street copies of their music that circulated in Bodegas, and self-production.

The departure of Grand Puba from their ranks; the potent message behind their graphic lyrics; personal and spiritual beliefs, affiliations and faith; and the necessary Armageddon to save the planet from its impending socio-political revolution and class war.

Pete Rock & C.L. Smooth arrived on the scene with the release of the ***All Souled Out EP***, June 25, 1991, on Elektra Records. Embraced by aficionados from far and wide for the majestic production mastery of Pete Rock, the duo officially set themselves up with the got next tag.

Pete Rock & C.L. Smooth returned with the certified classic long player of Mecca and the Soul Brother on June 9, 1992. The featured interview occurred in Toronto before the release of ***Mecca and the Soul Brother***, in the basement of Toronto's legendary Concert Hall, with J. Alexander Ferron. Vibrations from the live show up above heard for the first six minutes of the conversation. C.L. Smooth spoke on Mecca as a way of life and its state of mind; the inspiration behind the lyrics; ghostwriting; the mechanics and thought to process behind their songwriting process; and the fallout from the recent Biz Markie sampling judgement. Pete Rock a.k.a. Soul Brother No. 1 and Chocolate Boy Wonder, stuck to the music stating "Every beat I do it has to be fat."

New York State of Mind 1.0 serves as a free digital download on all platforms to introduce you to the Behind The Music Tales series. There is a print version available for those of you who take advantage of the sensation of holding a paperback in your hands. There will be plenty more upcoming releases within the series. I hope you enjoy this one and return to check out more.

Disclaimer

Opinions expressed in the interviews are not necessarily those of the Author. A few are not socially acceptable or politically correct in this world, and many will not appreciate seeing them in print. However, they exist here as a historical document of the times.

CHAPTER 1

Tragedy Khadafi

Intelligent Hoodlum a.k.a. Tragedy Khadafi, born Percy Chapman on August 13, 1971, is about as real as it does when it comes to Queens, NY and its infamous Queensbridge Housing Projects. Known far and wide for his important MC skills and formidable reputation on the streets, he has unfortunately lived the life of a true hoodlum. In and out of incarceration for selling drugs and robbery, he has also been shot and stabbed and suffered broken noses and arms.

Tragedy began his career in rhyme as a pre-teen, alongside DJ Hotday, initially under the guidance of a man named Larry. He hustled his way up the MC ladder one step at a time by rhyming in parks, music seminar elevators, and clubs under the names of MC Jade and MC Percy before convincing his Queensbridge Houses neighbour Marley Marl to provide him with a chance. He then gradually worked his way towards becoming a certified junior member of the legendary Juice Crew alongside senior members Big Daddy Kane, Kool G. Rap and MC Shan, all while maintaining his street movements.

Found guilty of robbery at the age of 16, he served time in the maximum security state prison, Elmira Correctional Facility, where he was conscripted and indoctrinated by the Five-Percent Nation. He then released into public life as Intelligent Hoodlum.

The **Intelligent Hoodlum** album on A&M Records arrived on June 19, 1990, in the midst of a wave of enlightened conscious young artists seeking to spread the truth and knowledge their elders educated them. Produced by Marley Marl and Large Professor, its fierce salvos "Black & Proud", "Back to Reality" and "Arrest The President" was overt socio-political manifestos directed at uplifting poor Black youth and riling up the hardcore masses.

With fire in both his heart and eyes, Tragedy Khadafi worked hard in the studio to further teach and educate the streets recording a set of incendiary songs between 1991 and 1992 for an album tentatively titled **Black Rage**.

Unfortunately, the timing could not have been worse, as it coexisted with the infamous Ice-T and Body Count freedom of speech war that nearly took down the Time Warner empire. Sadly this work was rejected, remixed or wholly dropped due to its lyrical bombs.

Three years after the release of his debut album, Intelligent Hoodlum was selected to usher in the urban music A&M imprint, Tuff Break, with ***Tragedy: Saga of a Hoodlum*** on June 22, 1993. It was on point and potent but admittedly its powerful message was reigned in by a cadre of powers that be, label executives, retail and shareholders, due to the times. Marley Marl still had a hand in the production, but for the most part, the album featured new and unknown Producers on the come up.

In The Beginning

Ice: Marley Marl discovered your talent, right?

Tragedy Khadafi:
Well, to be honest, this other kid discovered me. His name was Hotday, well - Larry. Larry and Hotday really discovered me but then being that Marley was like the bigger guy, he was Marley Marl, so we more or less started messing with him, and he put me on as far as the label thing and getting a deal and stuff.

Ice: You were rapping on the Juice Crew All-Stars at the age of 14.

Tragedy Khadafi:

Yeah, 14.

Ice: I read you sneaked into the New Music Seminar, rhymed in the elevators and handed out cards.

Tragedy Khadafi:
Yeah, yeah, like when they had Kriss Kross and all that. I was real small doing that back in the days, but nobody was smart enough to capitalise on it. I said, "Look, we got our stuff here!" They wasn't thinking like that at the time. I would sneak in seminars, sneak in battle people. I ain't have a badge or nothing. I just got in. That's why if you want to do something you gonna do it. Nobody couldn't tell me I wasn't getting in that seminar, and any club I wanted to get into I always got into.

Somehow, someway. If I had to sneak in through a side door, give the bouncer $20, I was in there. I'm gonna be in the place to be.

Ice: How did you get hooked up with the Juice Crew?

Tragedy Khadafi:
Well, me and Larry got hooked up when I was going to the parks, and through Larry, I met Hotday, and Hotday was like, look ... See, I was young, and he was like Larry's not that good. You should get with me, blazhay blah, this and that. I was like aiight, whatever. I want to get on. So I got with Hotday but Hotday... He was like - Everything was like mainly my ideas. He was a good DJ and stuff, but he didn't know how to make beats. So that's where Marley came in the picture 'cause I was like "Yo, I need beats!" And Hotday was kinda scared for me to get with Marley 'cause he knew Marley would cut him out the picture and that's what happened 'cause Marley was like he could be a DJ. He don't have to sign with you, which was kind of true 'cause Hotday wanted to sign with me like he was an artist like myself but he was just a DJ, and I was like that's kinda true, so me and Marley became. And how I met Marley is he lived on my block, he lived on my street, and I would see him, whatever, try to kick it to him, but he would never really give me no play. So I just kept fucking with him, bothering him, so he finally just listened to me. He gave me a little shot to come to his crib. I went to his crib, and I wrote a new song that night. I stayed up memorising it, went to his crib, he liked it, put it on tape, and he shopped it. We got a deal on an independent label called NIA Records. Remember that song "Confusion/This is my brain/Confusion"? What about that song "Release Yourself"?

Well, the guy that made that song, Aleem, they owned NIA Records, and they gave me my first deal or whatever, but that shit went bad in like six months.

Ice: Did you come with anything on that?

Tragedy Khadafi:
Yeah, I came out with one single called "Coke Is It" [released as Super Kids "The Tragedy (Don't Do It")]. But that shit went bad in like six, seven months.

Ice: Then you just stayed with Marley and hooked up.

Tragedy Khadafi:
When that shit ain't work, I got kind of discouraged. Then I just started fucking around on the street getting in trouble and shit. That's when I got locked down. Then when I came home, that's when I got hooked up with Marley again. But it was fucked up because I would still go in the studio, but I'll be getting in a lot of shit. I was on Volume 1, In Control Volume 1, Marley's album, and when that shit came out I was locked up. Me and my friends was joking about that yesterday, Lord, 'cause me and Lord was locked up together, my man Lord, and he was like damn. We was joking about it yesterday. He was like "Damn! I remember when your shit dropped." We was on Riker's Island, and I used to have my Walkman and listen to my own shit on the radio when I was in jail. I was like "Damn!" I wouldn't want to listen to the whole thing. I'd listen to a little bit and take it off, and I didn't want to tell nobody 'cause I didn't want motherfuckers to be like "Yo! What the fuck you doing here, you got a song out." But then when I came home after that we hooked up, me and Marley hooked up again.

Ice: So he stayed in contact with you?

Tragedy Khadafi:
Yeah, a little something. Well, I had to stay in contact with him. He was really busy.

Ice: Then he was cool about the whole fact that. He just waited.

Tragedy Khadafi:
Yeah, definitely.

The Streets

Back in your early teenage years, you were known for committing ill things on the streets.

Tragedy Khadafi:
Yeah. I mean, my shit, yo. I mean, I did my thing, yo. I ain't tell customs that this morning though. They said, "Have you ever been in any trouble?" I said ... I was sleeping 'cause they had us in customs for like two hours. Not to get off the subject but I was laying on the little chairs in the airport sleeping. I was there sleeping 'cause I had a show last night, and I didn't get in until like 4 in the morning, and then we had to get up at 5:30 to come here. So, I'm dead tired, I'm at the airport, and the customs guy was like, "Well, have you ever been in trouble?" And I was like ... I snapped up and was like ... I said, "Yeah, yeah." He said, "Did you ever do any time?" I said, "Yeah, I think about six months. I was a Juvenile." He said, "What was it?" I said I got into a fight.

That wasn't the real story 'cause I just came home from jail in '89. I did like two-and-half years, almost three years, so I just told him that. I didn't want them to be like, 'Well, you know, you've been a felon, and we've got to look this up and check you out. You coming in this State or whatever, this country.' So that's what I told him but ... I did my little shit, but that shit taught me a lot, man. Every time I look at my fucking hand I'll be like yo I got to chill. I got to maintain. My shit is fucked up. I got stabbed in my hand and then my back. See this finger?

Ice: It ain't right.

Tragedy Khadafi:
Yeah, it ain't right. They cut a joint in my finger, and it can't stay straight. It's crooked. So, every time I look at my hand, it reminds like ... yo; got to stay on point. Word up.

How did that happen?

Tragedy Khadafi:
I was up at a High-School that I used to always go up to, and I robbed a kid. It was funny 'cause when I robbed him, he was with his girlfriend. He's a Colombian kid, a big drug dealer kid, and I robbed him, and most of the time when I used to rob people they would like say something like "Come on, man! Don't take my shit! Come on!" But I robbed this kid and he didn't say nothing. He just looked at me. He took his jewellery off; he put it in my hand! He gave me his wallet and everything. He took his girl's jewellery off and gave it to me. So, I was like ha ... I ran. I'm like ha, I did my thing, whatever.

A few days later I went back up there. So I'm talking to this girl and shit, right. I'm talking to her just kicking it, and she starts screaming. So I'm like, "Yo, what's wrong with you?" She just kept screaming. I turned around I see Money running up on me like this with a knife. So my reflexes, 'cause I used to box, my reflexes, I threw my hands up in my face, and he stabbed me in my hand. Then he pulled the shit out, and I tried to run, and he caught me in my back. Boom! In my back! So then I fell, and then the ill shit is he fucking had a gun, but up in New York, up at the High-Schools, they have Cops up there at each corner.

Not at each corner but on one side of the school will be a Cop and on the other side of the school will be a Cop 'cause sometimes there's a lot of fights. So a Cop came, but if that Cop didn't come he would have fuckin' shot me, and I couldn't understand why he fuckin' would stab me if he had a gun, but it was like he wanted to really hurt me, and that's how that shit went. Word up.

What do you think about Young MC and Fresh Prince now coming out hardcore and wearing the gear, trying to look hardcore and watering it down?

Tragedy Khadafi:
I don't know about Young MC. I never was really into him but Fresh Prince, to me Fresh Prince he never tried to come hardcore. He's always been a funny kind of Rapper, a Comedian, a comedic Rapper. I like his music. I can't front on him 'cause I remember his first show in New York. Marley took me to his first show and Ice-T's first show at Studio 54. That was downtown. That was Ice-T's first show in New York, and that was the Fresh Prince's first show in New York, and I always liked Fresh Prince from "Girls of the World Ain't Nothing But Trouble". To me, he never tried to be something he wasn't. Young MC, I never really got into him in the first place. I didn't like his stuff, but he's cool or whatever.

To me, I like all different kinds of Rappers. I'll listen to Biz 'cause Biz got some funny shit, but then Biz will flip and make a hardcore joint. He just won't be saying it's hardcore, but it'll have a hardcore feel, like "The Funk is Back". That's like a hardcore underground type of joint. But then he can flip and make some shit like "Let Me Turn You On" and that's cool.

I ain't out to diss nobody 'cause there's too much money in this game. Everybody can get their money be real with your shit. Don't come out one minute trying to be a Pimp and then trying to be fuckin' hardcore. Just be real with your shit.

The Message

The album is hard. You're killing the President.

Tragedy Khadafi:

No question. No question. Not just the President, the Presidents, the whole shit. Like my man said, 'How can a Duck give birth to a Chicken?' A Duck doesn't have the system to produce a Chicken.

You're referring to corporate America.

Tragedy Khadafi:
No question. How could corporate America, the government, how could they produce a better situation for people when it was designed to feed off people, feed off poor people, and make rich people richer? If this world was fair, then everybody would have the same amount of everything.

How I label, this album is it's a lesson in how to survive in and on the streets.

Tragedy Khadafi:
Mmmmm. I would say this album is not just one thing. It's a lot of things. I would say this album is like walking inside of my mind, like as if my mind was like a big theatre or museum or something 'cause it's just a lot of characteristics of myself, things, my viewpoints, my taste and my opinion on things 'cause some people may not feel like that.

Some people may not feel like Cops are bad. Some people may not feel like the government is not run by a bunch of snakes. They may feel like shit is right; Cops are right; Government is right. So everybody has their different opinion.

This album is like the story of a Hoodlum. How a Hoodlum is going to see things. A Hoodlum is gonna find himself incarcerated; A Hoodlum is gonna find himself on drugs, selling drugs; A Hoodlum is gonna find himself getting shot at, getting stabbed, getting his nose broke, getting his arm broke; A Hoodlum is gonna go through these type of things. So, it's like the story of a Hoodlum, what he's gonna go through.

You use some Five-Percenter terminology on the album. You have "Shalom a Leck" and say "As-salamu Alaykum" on the album. Are you a Five-Percenter?

Tragedy Khadafi:
I'm universal. I deal with all aspects. I'm universal. You could call me a Muslim 'cause a Muslim means one of peace. Mu means one. Asalaam means peace, a state of peace, at peace. Even though sometimes I flip. If you bring it, I'm a bring it to you too, like any normal human being would. The Five-Percenters, a lot of things the Five-Percent deal with I agree with too, like do for self. I deal with all of it. I'm universal. I'm not in one specific sector. I take truth from everything. Some things the Christians practice I believe. A true Christian is a true Muslim. Any Muslim or a true Christian they'll tell you that. To me, religion is a business. If you get caught up in it, you'll be a victim. I try to lead myself the best way I can.

I'm gonna make a lot of mistakes 'cause I'm a young man but I'm learning, and maybe one day I'll be a wise man.

Are you surprised at all the transformations your life has gone?

Tragedy Khadafi:
In a way. In a lot of ways I am, but then in a lot of ways, I'm not. I know I was meant to be here and I ain't trying to go out. I know the things, the changes I'm gonna go through in life is for a reason. It's gonna make me the man to where nobody can't fuck with me. You gonna have to look me in my face to fuck with me. You not gonna be fucking with me behind my back 'cause you just gonna know don't fuck with him. He ain't having that shit.

Bullet

This album took too long to be released. You had "Fuck Bush", and it was pulled, due to the timing.

Tragedy Khadafi:
Bush already got fucked. I didn't have to fuck him, hahaha. He already got fucked. The reason why I took so long with this album is because we had to change a little of the production 'cause some of the production was like getting prehistoric. In Hip-Hop the shit changes so fast. You got to go with the shit. If you don't go with it, you gonna be behind.

You had a problem with A&M and the song "Bullet".

Tragedy Khadafi:
True, true. A Cop song. It was a Cop song. It was like a revenge song on Cops. At first, everybody was with it, but then the Ice-T situation came about, whereas he bailed out. Not putting it on him but he bailed out on a situation and then it kind of messed everybody up like me, Kool G. Rap, Apache, Boo-Yaa T.R.I.B.E, a lot of us.

The Boo-Yaa had "Shoot 'Em Down".

Tragedy Khadafi:
Yeah, yeah. It messed a lot of people up, but I took it off the album trying to get to A to Z, so I took it off. It ain't dead though. It ain't dead. I'm gonna put it out.

You're going to earn loot off this album and then put it out yourself, or give it away free at shows?

Tragedy Khadafi:
Yep, give it away free, and I'm gonna put it out.
Let's hear some verses from that. What kind of stuff are you kicking in that song?

Tragedy Khadafi:
Mr. Officer you better not touch me/I got a fat nine and my nine ain't rusty/You can catch a bul-let if you want to play hero/A hero ain't nothing but a sandwich/Zero/So put away your badge 'cause your badge ain't shit/I'm picking up the 'Mack and then I'm stuffing in the clip/The bullets that I'm licking put a ripping in your vest/You open up your mouth now I'm a open up your chest.

Fucking with a brother cause a brother is Black/I got a little something that'll keep you off my back/ Gat gat gat goes the Glock when I rip/You faggot ass Cops better get off that shit/'Cause nowadays you Pigs are gonna end up dead/Spittin' up guts with a bullet in your head.

Ice: I read an article. I think it was The Source dissing Ice-T. It said that he should have come out and declared "Cop Killer" was Heavy Metal and not Hip-Hop. What do you think?

Tragedy Khadafi:
I think if he would have said that it would have got over. When you talk about Hip-Hop, people automatically think of young Black kids with guns. In the States or where I'm from anyway. When you mention Hip-Hop, they think of young Black kids going crazy with guns. So, if you make a Hip-Hop Cop killing song they gonna think of young Black kids with guns going out to kill Cops, but if he would have flipped it and said it was a Heavy Metal song it would have been a whole different repertoire. It would have been a whole different agenda.

What is your feeling about being on A&M after they said you could put it out but not with us?

Tragedy Khadafi:
Well, at first, I'm not gonna lie, I was kinda like oh shit! That's that shit! But then as I thought and as I kicked it with not just A&M, with other people, like other artists that I know, getting different opinions, like Chuck D, and he said something that was very important. He said, 'When you make songs like that you got to be able to take the repercussions that come behind it like possible threats on your life; death threats; people following you; tapping your phone. Things like that you got to take into consideration.' And he said, 'We being in this time that we in, this day and time if something happened to Tragedy and they put in the papers "Tragedy choked on a fishbone", the public is gonna say Tragedy choked on a fishbone.' Not knowing that the F.B.I., C.I.A., murked me, and nobody is gonna follow up and question it.

Ice: You would be a dead man.

Tragedy Khadafi:
Exactly. So I said, 'Yo, you right.' I'll do it, but I'll do it in another way, and I'll do it when I'm financially strong and physically strong, so when beef come to me, I can handle it. If I was deep like Farrakhan that'd be different 'cause he got a whole army. When he says move, it's gonna be time to move. I roll for solo. Somebody could be right on the next roof – bow! Right in the back of my head. I'm out. I'm out. That's how I got to look at it.

Plans

What's the broad picture for you?

Tragedy Khadafi:
The large picture for me is just winning the whole shit, winning the whole game. I'm gonna be the best I can be regardless. Tragedy is gonna be Tragedy regardless. I'm gonna talk about things that's on my mind. I'm gonna talk about the way I feel about certain things, and I'm gonna be Tragedy. And in doing that I'm gonna handle business, and I'm gonna take care of business, and I'm gonna put on other artists like myself and help them to where nobody helped me, and I'll guide them the way I'm being guided now.

Ice: Do you have plans to start your label or management company?

Tragedy Khadafi:
Right now, I got a clique called 25 to Life. It consists of a few groups that I'm working with like Maniac Men, my man Scramble, and a Producer called Domingo. He did tracks for Eric B & Rakim. We just got a family thing and we all down and we all work together and help each other out. As far as a label thing, I work very closely with Tuff Break Records, a new Hip-Hop label. They like to call it a street label, but I like to call it a Hip-Hop label 'cause that's what it is. To me, what's a street label? It's a Hip-Hop label, a Rap label.

Ice: Are you like an A&R bringing them groups?

Tragedy Khadafi:
I work sort of like an A&R, and also I work sort of like a Road Manager with the groups. In any area, in every area that the A&R work with. I take them around, introduce them to the people I know and make sure they're well connected. I also do a few tracks with the groups and write for the groups. It's like a real family thing. We got one of the biggest Producers that we just recently did a deal with, Jinx. So Tuff Break is gonna be on the map, and it's gonna be a major entity in Hip-Hop.

Are you planning to put out an album like the one Marley Marl put out?

Tragedy Khadafi:
A compilation? We was discussing that a few days ago. It's funny that you ask that. We were discussing a Tuff Break compilation, so most likely being that usually everything we talk about we manifest it, it just takes a minute. I think you should be looking forward to a fat Tuff Break EP compilation type of thing with Jinx, Babalou Bad; it got a real ill sort of hard but comedic flow to it, real cliché type of flow, straight G; Dred Scott; myself. So we got a nice little squad.

Will A&M distribute it?

Tragedy Khadafi:
Yes, definitely. Most definitely.

This album right now is old to you.

Tragedy Khadafi:
This one right now? It's not old. I mean, it's been done for a while but it's not old.

I mean, it's been done for a while but it's not old. It needs to be out there right now. It doesn't need to slowly be out there, it needs to be out there 'cause in a minute it will be old, but I'm working on the next one and I'm working on remixes to flavourize it for now, and I don't feel bad about that because those type of things happen, a lot, especially when you got to do shit right. You got to clear samples. You got to work a few things out, so shit takes time. The pace in Hip-Hop is faster than it ever was being that you got a lot of groups out there. Some are fat. Some are bullshit. I'm coming with the next shit. I'm working on the next shit right now as we speak. As a matter of fact I might have to fly back. I was supposed to do some shit in L.A. with one of the acts from Tuff Break but I might have to fly back and fuck with my remixes and get ready for the next shit to drop.

Is that going to be with the help of Marley and K-Def?

Tragedy Khadafi:
Nah. The remixes be looking at Backspin.

What else do you want to add?

Tragedy Khadafi:
That again, Tuff Break is gonna blow up. We gonna be in the house.

G. Rap and Big Daddy Kane and all those guys?

Tragedy Khadafi:
I ain't trying to follow nobody. I'm trying to take my shit to another level. Writing, writing. See, I could play a part in all that but writing is the other shit. Writing is putting life into it. So I'm gonna put life into it. I might act in it also.

It depends on how it's structured but I'm writing a movie right now that's all real. It's not no gangster shit though. It's like a life type of story. Love. Drugs. Sex. Abuse. Pain. Joy. It's life. It's not a gangster movie. It's not a street movie. It's a life movie 'cause the shit you gonna see in this movie could happen to anybody, white, Black. It's about kids trying to survive without nothing, their survival and making it, and that's what that's going to be.

What's the title?

Tragedy Khadafi:

Token. A token is something that's just there to be there; it has no purpose. It's like a Black man working for what's that shit, Lloyds of London? It's like a Black man working for Lloyds of London. He has no purpose there. He's just there. No existence. His face is just there for face, so people can say Lloyds of London hired a Black man. So that's what that's going to be about.

Next

The final Intelligent Hoodlum song was issued on May 4, 1993. It was the title track for the Mario Van Peebles film **Posse**, "The Posse (Shoot 'em Up" based on the 1898 "Buffalo Soldiers" of the U.S. 10th Calvary Regiment, who fought in the Spanish-American war.

Tuff Break Records was shut down by A&M Records in February 1995 citing they were "disappointed with the label's inability to generate the same kind of success A&M has with its pop and alternative acts."

Intelligent Hoodlum served a higher purpose by strongly influencing future Queensbridge emcees Nas, Cormega, Havoc, Capone and Noreaga. Each went on to spread a militant state of mind message to the masses.

Tragedy Khadafi is envisaged as the mastermind behind the classic Capone-N-Noreaga album, **The War Report**, credited with reviving hardcore east coast Hip-Hop. He appears on eight songs notably "T.O.N.Y. (Top of New York)" and the vicious response to Tha Dogg Pound single "New York, New York" titled "L.A., L.A.". Sadly Noreaga cuts ties with Tragedy when Capone was released from prison, and they went to war, recording diss tracks and calling each other out for many years.

The documentary film **Tragedy: The Story of Queensbridge** was released on January 23, 2005.

The film covers the Queensbridge Housing Projects and the life and times of Tragedy Khadafi and includes Mobb Deep, Marley Marl, Capone, Noreaga and others. Tragedy Khadafi was charged with selling narcotics and sentenced to a maximum of four years in prison on December 27, 2007. He was granted early parole and released on June 23, 2010.

The crucial 1991-1992 Intelligent Hoodlum recordings that were scrapped due to the socio-political climate of the times were released as the two-part **Black Rage Demos** series in 2010 and 2015 by Diggers With Gratitude, Heavy Jewelz Records and Tragedy Khadafi's very own 25 To Life Entertainment and Iller Regime. Part 2 is the one place to hear his revenge song on Cops, "Bullet".

Out of the blue, a video for "T.M. (Message to Killa Black)" of the **Against All Odds** album released June 5, 2001, arrived on June 27, 2016. Its powerful message rings true to this day.

Album Discography

Intelligent Hoodlum

- **Intelligent Hoodlum-1990** (A&M/PolyGram Records)
- **Tragedy: Saga of a Hoodlum** - June 19, 1990 (A&M/PolyGram Records)

Tragedy Khadafi

- **Against All Odds** - June 5, 2001 (Gee Street/V2/BMG Records)
- **Still Reportin'...** - October 21, 2003 (Solid Records)
- **Thug Matrix** - October 4, 2005 (FastLife Records)
- **The Death of Tragedy** - June 18, 2007 (Traffic Entertainment/25 To Life Aura)
- **Thug Matrix 41-18** - February 12, 2008 (Money Maker Entertainment)
- **Q.U. Soldier** - February 12, 2008 (Money Maker Entertainment)
- **Endless Tragedies with J-Love** - April 28, 2009 (Money Maker Entertainment)
- **Lethal Weapon with Trez** - September 26, 2010 (Trez)

- **Thug Matrix 3** - September 20, 2011 (25 To Life Aura/Money Maker Entertainment)
- **Hood Father** - December 20, 2011 (25 To Life Aura)
- **Militant Minds EP with Blak Madeen** - September 20, 2012 (Leedz Edutainment)
- **Golden Era Music Sciences with Tragic Allies** - May 14, 2013 (Ill Adrenaline Records)
- **Pre Magnum Opus** - December 16, 2014 (25 To Life Aura)

Music Videos

Intelligent Hoodlum

- "Black and Proud"
- "Back to Reality"
- "Arrest The President"
- "Grand Groove"
- "Street" (Return of the Life remix)
- "The Posse (Shoot 'em Up)"

Tragedy Khadafi

- "Ill-luminous Flow"
- "T.M. (Message to Killa Black)"

CHAPTER 2

Brand Nubian

When Brand Nubian released the certified classic album, **All For One**, on December 4, 1990, it marked the emergence of a gritty crew of emcees who mixed party energy and conscious, militant lyrics with style, creativity and soulful abstract rhymes. Made up of Lord Jamar, Grand Puba, Derek X and DJ Alamo, Brand Nubian was either hitting up your girl and her friends, or schooling you on the Nation of Islam and its beliefs.

Politically charged, socially conscious and armed with the 120 lessons of the Five-Percent Nation, they immediately drew in like-minded young revolutionaries attracted by their strong views and message. By the time its fourth single "Slow Down" dropped, Brand Nubian and ***All for One*** had enchanted a nation of youth in need of truth, guidance and understanding.

Sadly, Grand Puba kicked off with Lord Jamar and Derek X in 1991, and he checked out of the group to begin a solo career taking DJ Alamo with him. Lord Jamar and Sadat X (formerly Derek X) took it with a grain of salt and declined to sit still. They recruited DJ Sincere and set to work on new Brand Nubian music. The "Punks Jump Up To Get Beat Down" single was issued on January 12, 1993, and it instantly caused a ruckus with its highly controversial homophobic content.

The powerful ***In God We Trust*** album followed on February 2, 1993. Brand Nubian came back, and this time there was no mistaking the message. The strong lyrical message and undertone of the album reflected on the group's identity as Five-Percenters and the philosophy of the Nation of Gods and Earth. Dealing with equality and knowledge for their brothers and sisters, Brand Nubian possessed an active duty to educate and enlighten Black people back to nature and, the self.

Punks Jump Up To Get Beat Down

New York City earned a fierce worldwide reputation as a bootlegger base camp and paradise. Whether you wanted a taste or quantity of any hot brand, it was well there for the taking, or shipping, at a fraction of the manufacturers suggested retail price. Anything and everything from purses and apparel to fragrances, watches and jewellery, its lowest priced and fastest moving products were prerecorded mixtapes, new films, porn, and, of course, that hot new Hip-Hop album by your favourite artists and groups. The rise in popularity of Hip-Hop made it lucrative for eager bootleggers who wanted their piece of the pie, and every new album distributed to a cut-rate and easily accessible for those in the know.

Dru Silver: How do you feel about the bootlegs?

Lord Jamar:
Not happy about it. We made a song on the new album addressing it and shit got to stop.

Dru Silver: You live in New York. What do you do when you see the bootleggers?

Lord Jamar:
See, they're not the bootleggers. They're the ones that's selling it, but they're not producing it. On the last album, we went out there and then took our tapes like everybody else, threatening motherfuckers and shit. That shit is not solving nothing.

Sadat X:

They buy the tapes legit. They buy them from a wholesale place.

Lord Jamar:

Somebody at a higher level. Those are the ones; you got to go and break them up, not the ones on the street. That don't make no sense.

You got Diamond D on "Punks Jump Up To Get Beat Down", but you did most of your production.

Lord Jamar:

Yeah, we did everything.

Sadat X:

Everything on the album except for that and with "Punks" we worked with Diamond. We had a hand in everything on the album. He just did that one, and we helped him out but other than that we did the whole thing, everything; beats, rhymes, everything.

Where do you find your stuff?

Sadat X:

Wherever, we see records on the street. We went to a record store today in Toronto; we got some beats. Just from wherever. We accumulate them. We got stacks of records. We find them wherever.

Dru Silver: You are Brand Nubian brothers, but you made a song like "Punks Jump Up To Get Beat Down". What's behind that?

Lord Jamar:
It's all about being real. It's part of reality, a lot of symbolism. It's like, we positive and all that but you can't let no person take advantage of you no matter what colour they are; Black, white, blue. If they violate, somethings got to happen. If someone tries to take your life, you got to defend yourself no matter what colour they are, and so we address a lot of that this album, but it's not like we're on any specific Black on Black violence and anything like that. We talking about anybody.

Business

Dru Silver: Everybody in Toronto wants to get in the Hip-Hop business, and the Record business is fucking hard, period. What advice will you give them?

Lord Jamar:
Work hard. If you know you got the talent, and if you know you can do it, and this is what you're supposed to do. But that don't mean just running up on every Hip-Hop kid you see and be like "Yo! I can rhyme! I want you to listen to me and put me on!" That's not the way it's done. I've been wanting to make a record for years and years since I was very young rhyming, and I used to go to a lot of jams, and I used to see people that was my idols, but I never ran up on 'em or was like "Yo! Put me on! Put me on!" because there's a certain — you can't do that. You look and be like inspired by them, be like I'm not gonna run up on him. He's gonna know me someday and boom bam! I'm gonna work for that. You do need a form of connections, but if you work and make yourself known somebody will step to you type thing, and that's what happened with me, and that's what happened with X. We didn't run after nobody. Somebody stepped to us after we went out there and grabbed mics at every block party, at every house party and High-School parties, and somebody finally stepped up and was like "Yo! I think your shit is fly and let's do something."

Dru Silver: Will Brand Nubian be producing for other people in the future?

Lord Jamar:
I don't think like in a way like Pete Rock be doing it something but in a way ...

Dru Silver: If somebody comes up to you and says, I like your beats -

Lord Jamar:
Nah. I think, if we see something in somebody and they're saying exactly what we want to hear, or if we found a group that we felt we was going to put them out or whatever, we'd do that. But as far as just people saying we want beats from y'all just so they could sell a bunch of records and play yourself out, we're not trying to get into that realm. We're keeping the beats for ourselves.

There was much time in-between releases.

Lord Jamar:
Yeah, it was, but that's 'cause the first album it was lasting for so long. People was playing it for a long time. We was working like a year straight just off that album, just doing shows.

Grand Puba

What went down with Puba? Why did he leave?

Lord Jamar:
Just musical differences. You listen to his new album; you listen to our album; his album is more playful and more happy, and our album is more serious and more just a different feeling, and that was reflective of the mindset of what we were on and what he was on.

Dru Silver: When I listen to your album, it's more like what kids nowadays want to hear. When you listen to Puba's its sit down and relax music.

Lord Jamar:
That also goes to he's older than us. He's almost 30 years old. It's like, we're 24 years old. We're coming from - We down with the old school now, we ain't new to this, but at the same time we down with the new school, as far as we know what the people our age want to hear. He's getting to a point in his life where he's gonna make something to kick back and can't do as much energy or whatever because you get older and start to look at things different. We just ... The way we came is we see the way things is going on the street and all that and the sound that's happening, and we just rolling where we feel right. That's about it.

Puba does not comment on it. He says something deep went down, and I heard something went down in San Francisco.

Lord Jamar:
Ain't nothing that happened outside of New York. It's nothing big. It ain't nothing that really anybody needs to know about. It doesn't matter what went down. It's just that it went down and this is the best for everybody. Exactly what happened, the world doesn't need to know that. Everybody's happy now. It's not like someone had to suffer like we broke up and now somebody's poor, and somebody's on. We both straight, so let's leave it at that.

Faith

Are you Islamic?

Lord Jamar:
Islam; we're Islamic but not in a traditional orthodox sense of praying five times a day type of Islam or anything, or thinking that God is in the sky or anything. Our Islam is I, Self, Lord and Master, which is me, which is Self. Islam within Self. Islam is a way of life as your natural way to do things, not like as a religion.

Who schooled you in the Black man teachings and Allah's word?

Lord Jamar:
Just from around the way. There's one particular brother who used to sit me down when I was young and explain certain things to me about life, about the Black man, about the white man, about all people and answered a lot of different questions that I always had in my mind and just sparked it from there. But you the only one that can accept it. Somebody can tell you, but you have to accept it for yourself.

Are you still learning?

Lord Jamar:
You learn every day. Knowledge is infinite. No one will know everything. Knowledge has no limitations.

Do you want separation?

Lord Jamar:
Yeah, I think separation is good. I think Black people need to get with themselves first before they try to get with anyone else because ... for the simple fact that ... I don't know how the curriculum and stuff goes down over here. I can only imagine it's not far from how it is in America. In America, the Black man is taught to hate the Black man and to hate his Blackness and to hate himself. I don't think that we can go out here loving any other people 'till we learn how to love ourselves as a people. I didn't make that philosophy up, but it's a philosophy that I agree with. That's just a reality of life. A lot of people want it to be different, but it can't be different until certain steps are taken. You can't build a house without having a foundation first. You want to build the third floor, but you got to get the first and second floor first.

Dru Silver: How do you feel about kids wearing Malcolm X clothes, white kids and Black kids, when a lot of them don't know what he did?

Lord Jamar:
They're wearing it.

Muslims are being attacked all over the world, in India and Iraq right now. How do you feel about white Muslims being killed by the Serbians?

Lord Jamar:
I don't know too much about that. I'm a Black man in America, and I can't speak on what's going on in other

parts of the world that I'm not ... Well, it might affect me indirectly but I'm not there to know exactly the details of what's going on, and I don't trust the media, what they say, so, I'm worried about the people that's in my direct midst.

Do you acknowledge them and what's going on there?

Lord Jamar:
I mean, I don't know what's going on. I don't know. I'm not keeping up on that right now.

What do you think about Rastafarians?

Lord Jamar:
I think they trying to get back to their original selves. It's like each person sometimes has different practices on how they do things but could still be going for the same thing. We all getting ready to eat food but I might use chopsticks, you might use a fork, or you can use a spoon, but we all gonna get fed, and no one way is better than the other way. I feel that Rastafarians have a lot of positive - I learn a lot from Rastafarians.

They're a cult of Christianity. They took the Bible and their beliefs and translations of it and made their religion. Would you say that Five-Percenters did that with the Koran? *(uneducated statement and question #1)

Lord Jamar:
We don't study the Koran in the Five Percent Nation. We study the 120 Lessons, which is lessons that were written by WD Farhad and Honourable Elijah Mohammad, which are given to the Nation of Islam, who run the rules of the Nation of Islam. Christianity, the original Christianity was started

by Black people. Christianity that's being practised now is not the original Christianity. The Rastafarians goes into the Bible and reveal the truth that's in the Bible. We do that within the Five Percent Nation also. We go into the Bible and reveal the truth. We go into the Koran and reveal the truth, but we don't study each one as our foundation doctrine. Our foundation is Mathematics and the 120 Lessons.

Would you say that you are one of Allah's children?

Lord Jamar:
I'd say that I'm Allah. I'd say I am Allah. Along with all the other brothers that think like me.

Allah's children are not permitted to swear. You cannot pray and curse out of the same mouth. Why do you swear? ** (uneducated statement and question #2)

Lord Jamar:
Once again, you're going into orthodox Muslim doctrine. Something that was written thousands of years ago and each culture or religion is fashioned to the environment and times that you're in. This is 1993. If you're a Muslim, you're supposed to be wearing white robes and praying three times a day, not cursing, like you said, and not drinking these brews. That's bullshit. This is 1993. I can't get my point across to my brothers and sisters like I need to if I'm coming with white robes and I'm all spooky, and I'm not swearing, and I'm talking all proper. You take what I'm saying better if we share a brew together and we just kicking it, and I'm talking the same way you talking. You're gonna relate to me better.

If I come to you as someone of thousands of years ago, here in 1993, you're gonna look at me like I'm a crazy man.

Dru Silver: It goes in one ear and out the other.

Lord Jamar:
That's what I'm saying. You're gonna be obsessed with me looking the way I look and the way I'm talking. This is just reality. This language is not even our language as Black people anyway. We're speaking English. I'm not an Englishman. I'm not from England, even though I'm speaking English. So, it's like no word to me - I redefine my words. No word in this language I don't take it for what they tell me it is. We use it for what we want to use it for. So, no word is any more superior or any harsher than me than any other word.

You refer to the Devil a lot. Who is the Devil?

Lord Jamar:
The Devil is the white man in planet Earth. The Devil is also some Black people. The Devil is the graphic mentality. Once you get to your weakest point, mentally as well as physically, that's the Devil. There's a lot of Black people whose grafted themselves mentally as the Devil. As Elijah Mohammad has taught us, and as Master Farhad Mohammad taught him ... As Elijah Mohammad taught us, the physical Devil of this planet Earth is indeed the Caucus Asian. The one from the caucus mountains, the white man in planet Earth, and this is what we teach, and these are my understanding and belief. This is what I know to be reality.

Do you preach education with equality?

Lord Jamar:
Preach education with equality? Yeah, but when I say equality you might not know what I mean. I mean, equality is to deal in equally in all forms of knowledge. I deal equality with my brothers and sisters by rhyming this knowledge.

Am I not included?

Lord Jamar:
I mean, are you a Caucasian?

I'm white.

Lord Jamar:
Well, it tells us in our lessons that we teach freedom, justice and equality to all human families of the planet earth but my duty is amongst my people, which are Black people. Those are the ones that I direct my message too, and I understand a lot of people, white people like our music and all that stuff, and like what we're saying, but we making it for Black people, and the message that we give is for Black people. Not saying that white people can't benefit from it. If they listen, they could benefit from it, but it's not for them.

***

I do not claim to possess knowledge beyond a basic understanding of Brand Nubian's background, militant and socio-political conscious lyrics. At the time I had read a few articles and LeRoi Jones a.k.a. Amiri Baraka books and listened to a few people in my circle speak. Was it enough to connect with Brand Nubian and the profound social meaning behind their educational survival songs? I thought so at the time.

Hindsight is always 20/20, and a lot of my questions loaded. Looking back 23 years later this must be addressed, and a few of the responses. I contacted Salman 'Ylook' Rana, Hip-Hop Head, Scholar, Lawyer, and asked for his thoughts on a few of the questions and answers you see here.

Salman Rana:

I'm assuming at the time that Lord Jamar was young, his ideas re the 5% (and the 5% Nation itself as an intellectual thing) were still developing. But firstly, some thoughts on what it means to be an 'orthodox' Muslim. Again, I think this is a loaded term that itself comes with a number of assumptions that may not necessarily be accurate.

1. Muslims don't generally refer to themselves as 'God's children.' This comes more from Judeo-Christian (more Christian than Jewish in fact) thought and dogma. Muslims view themselves as vicegerents, representatives and in the mystical (metaphysical sense) 'slaves', taken non-pejoratively, and in a more liberatory sense.

    There is no specific Muslim dress, outside of the requirements of modesty and humility. There is traditional attire, but this is subject to culture. Thus, a Muslim from Senegal will wear traditional attire that will differ from a Muslim from the Gulf, that will differ from a Muslim from the Indian Subcontinent, that will differ from a Muslim from Bosnia, etc. Do Muslims share different traditional clothing? Of course. In the American context, many Muslims in the African American community for example, because of their travel and exposure to Muslim institutions and resources in the Gulf states, generally adopted traditional dress from those places. But we see very real differences in outward expressions of Muslim dress from other African American communities that travelled to Senegal and Morocco for traditional learning.

3. Praying and Swearing: Muslims aren't perfect, and Islam isn't a utopian faith. It recognises the dystopic nature of everyday life, and individuals figure centrally into that dystopia. Muslims practice and identify with their faith in varying degrees. You have lay Muslims, who like others, struggle with their faith in the context of their surroundings, and with the innumerable contradictions that anyone else has to negotiate in their day to day lives, whether that be using expletives, drinking alcohol, dating, etc. The virtue is in the struggle to stay on the moderate path (the middle ground), and to attain a relative level of goodness in their daily lives (through their relationships with others, behaviour, thoughts, ideas, goals, health, etc.). Even Mevlana Rumi swore in his quatrains and parables! The difference here is that a Muslim struggling with any number of contradictions won't justify those contradictions, but recognise them as shortcomings to address and overcome in an effort to perfect their lives in accordance with the spiritual path they choose to take up.

4. Situating Islamic doctrine (which is complex and runs through several disciplines such as mysticism, theology, law, jurisprudence and philosophy), as something that is simply fixed 1,400 years ago, is also incorrect. It is a living tradition, that has developed over the course of time, and continues to respond to the challenge of tradition and modernity.

While there are fixed principles in the normative doctrine, i.e. the oneness of God, much of it, like law, for instance, is active and malleable. Much like he said, "culture and religion are fashioned to the time", and this continues to be the case.

5. On being able to communicate with people, he's right. You have to speak to people in a way that relates to and resonates with them. But I don't think this necessitates things like misogyny and alcohol, whether you're a Muslim or not. Just respect. And again, like mentioned above, normative Islam wouldn't make justifications for the consumption of something like alcohol as a means to better adapt to a particular cultural climate or foster better communication.

I think the issue of the 5% Nation as heterodox Islam is a dead letter now. I think what we know is that they emerge from the American Muslim experience as negotiated by the African American community, through an appropriation of Islamic terminology and rhetoric, but fashioning something entirely different. Lord Jamar released an album years ago, in which he had a short book outlining the nature of the 5%. In which he clearly states that the 5% are not Muslim - but when you listen to Brand Nubian's, 'Wake Up', Puba asks, "Can the Devil Fool a Muslim?" - Which may confuse readers and listeners. If you go back to Poor Righteous Teachers' first record, the association with traditional Islam is even stronger. So I think you have to understand 5% Nation's doctrine through a developmental spectrum, through which they've arrived at a point in their intellectual development where they see themselves as something clearly distinct from what might be framed as normative Islam.

There are a couple of good books written on them now for further reference:

- Felicia Miyazawa, **Five Percenter Rap: God Hop's Music, Message, and Black Muslim Mission** (Bloomington: Indiana University Press, 2005)
- Michael Muhammad Knight, **The Five Percenters: Islam, Hip-Hop and the Gods of New York** (Oneworld Publications, 2008)
- Michael Muhammad Knight, **Why I Am a Five Percenter** (TarcherPerigee, 2011)

Revolution

"Black Star Line" is about Marcus Garvey's steamship company.

Lord Jamar:
Kind of. It's about a mental Black Star Line.

The song is about his abilities and his ideas -

Lord Jamar:
It's about - it's letting people know a basic history about Marcus Garvey.

That he was around and what his idea was.

Lord Jamar:
Right, and trying to relay that in terms of today on a mental Black Star Line. Free your mind. Get aboard and free your mind. Not necessarily having to physically go back to Africa but to mentally get back to your true nature and your true self, and that's what we talking about.

Did he not raise the monies under false pretence to run that company?

Dru Silver: Who says that?

Lord Jamar:
Word. Who did say that?

I read that somewhere but do not recall where.

Lord Jamar:
I've never heard that.

I know he sold shares.

DJ Sincere:
I believe that they indicted him.

Lord Jamar:
You can be indicted. That don't mean that you did it.

DJ Sincere:
Especially in those times. You don't understand, in those times the F.B.I. was working against any progress that Black people had to make. There were many accusations about different Black leaders into corruption and different things.

Lord Jamar:
And you know what, me personally, I don't care if he did scam to get the money. You know why? Because the ex-slaves - Liberia in Africa was settled by the ex-slaves of the United States, you understand? They went back to Africa. They did what they had to do, and I don't care if the man did scam the money or not, to tell you the truth, because he was doing it for a good cause, but I don't believe that's true. But if he did, I don't fault him for it.

DJ Sincere:
Something had to be done.

Lord Jamar:
Yep! Nobody else was doing it.

Ice-T says the revolution will come from the white kids.

Lord Jamar:
Oh yeah? I didn't know that.

Any comments about that?

Lord Jamar:
Revolution means change. Change is gonna happen for everybody real soon. Whether you like it or not. That's right.

What's going to happen?

Lord Jamar:
A lot of things. America got its own little revolution that they think they're gonna put you through, and not just America, the world has a little plan they want to put all people through now, but I got a little plan that I want to put them through.

Which is?

Lord Jamar:
Which is Armageddon?

Why?

Lord Jamar:
Why? 'Cause it's necessary.

DJ Sincere:
To defeat the plan that they have.

Lord Jamar:
That's right. Or else we gonna be dead.

Are you speaking about Black people?

Lord Jamar:
Yep. Maybe white people too. Oh, they gonna kill you too. They will kill you too. See, for all these years they've been just against the Black people. Now watch. It's not gonna be Black or white. It's gonna be rich and poor.

Sadat X:
See all them programs now in New York?

Lord Jamar:
It's gonna be the rich against the poor, and those who cooperate against those who don't cooperate. That's what it's gonna be.

So, rich against poor all with the object of getting money and more power?

Lord Jamar:
It's gonna be the rich wanting to control the poor. That's what it is, and they're doing it now, but it's gonna be blatant.

In how long will this occur?

Lord Jamar:
Oh, about six years.

Where did you get that number from?

Sadat X:
From our research.

Lord Jamar:
What we've been studying. Why I think? Because that will be the year 1999.

Sadat X:
Different programs, like the thing now. They're teaching the gay stuff to young kids in school. All that's part of the program.

Lord Jamar:
A lot of people don't realise.

What's wrong with being gay?

Lord Jamar:
'Cause it's against the laws of nature. It don't make sense.

Dru Silver: God didn't create Adam and Steve.

Lord Jamar:
Yeah! Sex is for reproduction, for creation, not recreation. You're wrecking your creation when you're sticking your dick in somebody's ass; fuckin' sickies.

Knowledge Is Power

"Pass The G.A.T." G.A.T. means God Allah's Truth?

Lord Jamar:
Yep, and it means gun.

So you are saying knowledge is as or more powerful than a gun?

Lord Jamar:
Hell yeah! How you gonna make a gun if you don't know how.

DJ Sincere:
Exactly. It's the foundation of all things in the system.

Lord Jamar:
Without knowledge there is nothing. Nothing would exist.

Why do kids have to listen to groups like you? Why don't they go and research it by themselves? Why does it take Rappers to get kids looking into themselves?

Sadat X:
Because a lot of the times it's been phased out already, and they don't know nothing about it.

Lord Jamar:
They've been taught to not even - They don't know that there's something to look for sometimes. They think that how everything is how it's supposed to be.

Sadat X:
They don't know about Marcus Garvey. They know about Martin Luther King. They don't know about Marcus Garvey. They know about George Washington.

Lord Jamar:
They know about George Washington.

Sadat X:
Thomas Jefferson.

DJ Sincere:
Columbus.

Sadat X:
They don't know about a man from Milwaukee, the Black Panthers there.

Lord Jamar:
And then they don't even know the full story on those people though.

What's the full story?

Lord Jamar:
That half the Presidents of the United States was Masons and all kind of secret orders going on and -

DJ Sincere:
Slave Masters.

Lord Jamar:
And fucking George Washington was a slave owner and all that type of shit. They don't tell you that shit.

Sadat X:
One of the biggest slave owners.

DJ Sincere:
But they stood for freedom and justice and equality.

Lord Jamar:
Truth, honour and justice. The American way.

Sadat X:
They tell you that Kennedy was a great President, but they don't tell you that his Pops bootlegged liquor in the depression; he was the number one bootlegger in the United States.

Summing up Brand Nubian, would you say that you are about songs of survival?

Sadat X:
Songs of life.

Lord Jamar:
Yeah, I'd say songs of survival, songs of reality, songs of education. Education for survival. There you go. Educational survival songs. There you go. Write that down.
Educational Survival Songs Volume 1..

Next

Brand Nubian recorded "Lick Dem Muthaphuckas" for inclusion on the **Menace II Society** soundtrack released on May 26, 1993.

The third Brand Nubian album **Everything is Everything** was released on November 1, 1994. Single "Word Is Bond" did well but the album did not, and the group then went their separate ways. Sadat X signed with Loud Records as a solo artist and released **Wild Cowboys** on July 16, 1996. It sold on the strength of its title track, "Hang 'Em High" and "The Lump Lump," and is known for featuring a top-shelf assortment of Producers led by D.I.T.C. members Diamond D, Buckwild and Showbiz, Pete Rock and Da Beatminerz. Grand Puba participated on "Open Bar". A sequel album **Wild Cowboys II** was made public by Fat Beats on March 10, 2010.

Brand Nubian reunited with Grand Puba in 1997 and recorded "A Child Is Born" for the **Soul in the Hole** soundtrack, and "Keep It Bubblin'" for the **Money Talks** soundtrack culminating in the full-length Foundation album released on September 29,1998. "Don't Let It Go To Your Head" was their most successful single ever. The Neptunes remix featuring Kelis on background vocals,"Take It To Your Head," smashed inside clubs too.

The original group reunited again for the self-produced album **Fire In The Hole** released August 10, 2004.

Time's Running Out came on August 21, 2007, it was used as an outlet to issue more songs recorded in 1997 and 1998 for the Foundation album. Grand Puba and Sadat X recorded "Once Again (Here to Kick One For You)" on the Handsome Boy Modeling School album ***So... How's Your Girl*** released on October 19, 1999, by Tommy Boy Records. The pair reconvenes on the Just Blaze-produced "Bread & Butter" for the Beanie Sigel album ***The B. Coming*** released on March 29, 2005, by Dame Dash. Lord Jamar released his sole solo album, **The 5% Album**, on June 27, 2006. The entire album is dedicated to the message of the Five Percent Nations of Gods & Earths and comes complete with a 90-page booklet of illustrations, images, thoughts and documentation. The RZA, Chef Raekwon, Grand Puba and Sadat X contributed featured appearances.

Lord Jamar is a successful actor who has been on episodes of ***Oz, Third Watch, Law & Order: Special Victim's Unit, The Sopranos, Rescue Me, Elementary, and Person Of Interest*** to list a few. In 2016, he featured as Tino in six episodes of the critically acclaimed HBO crime and drama series ***The Night Of***. Vlad TV posted an exclusive interview with Lord Jamar on February 1, 2013, where he spoke of the sad state of Hip-Hop fashion and called out Kanye West for wearing a skirt. On February 4, 2013, he doubled-down with the Kanye West diss track "Lift Up Your Skirt," also released on Vlad TV. A frequent guest on Vlad TV, Lord Jamar has been described as a racist and homophobic for his words and views on life and Hip-Hop culture.

Grand Puba has released five studio albums. His most recent ***Black From The Future*** on April 15, 2016.

Sadat X has maintained his solo career with consistent releases on many labels. His 11th album, ***Agua***, was made public by Tommy Boy Records on July 15, 2016. His next album, ***The Sum of A Man***, is planned for December 23, 2016. It will be entirely produced by Diamond D and features Raheem Devaughn, Kurupt, Tha Liks, Blake Moses, Jawz of Life, Peter Wayne, and Timmy Hunter. This LP is the culmination of collaborations for the past two decades. Starting with "A Day in the Life" from Diamond D's classic ***Stunts Blunts and Hip Hop*** LP, to "You Can't Front," to Diamond's productions for "Punks Jump Up To Get Beat Down," and Sadat's ***Wild Cowboys*** album.

Album Discography

Brand Nubian

- **One for All** - December 4, 1990 (Elektra)
- **In God We Trust** - February 2, 1993 (Elektra)
- **Everything Is Everything** - November 1, 1994 (Elektra)
- **Foundation** - September 29, 1998 (Arista)
- **Fire in the Hole** - August 10, 2004 (Babygrande)
- **Time's Runnin' Out** - August 2, 2007 (Traffic Entertainment)
- **The Now Rule Files** - September 15, 2009 (One Leg Up)
- **Enter the Dubstep Vol. 2** - December 21, 2010 (Frank Radio)

Sadat X

- **Wild Cowboys** - July 15, 1996 (Loud/RCA)
- **The State of New York vs. Derek Murphy** - September 19, 2000 (Relativity Records)
- **Experience & Education** - October 25, 2005 (Female Fun Music)
- **Black October** - October 3, 2006 (Female Fun Music)
- **Generation X** - November 4, 2008 (Tell-X Records)

- **Brand New Bein'** - May 5, 2009 (Loud)
- **Wild Cowboys II** - March 23, 2010 (Fat Beats)
- **No Features** - July 4, 2011 (Tell-X Records)
- **Love, Hell or Right** - December 4, 2012 (6.8.2 Records)
- **True Wine Connoisseur's with Will Tell** - January 21, 2013
- **Never Left** - January 20, 2015 (Loyalty Digital Corp.)
- **Coast Connect with Fudra** - April 16, 2016 (Eggcart Productions)
- **Agua** - July 15, 2016 (Tommy Boy)

Lord Jamar

- **The 5% Album** - January 27, 2006 (Babygrande Records)

Grand Puba

- **Reel to Reel** - October 20, 1992 (Elektra)
- **2000** - June 20, 1995 (Elektra)
- **Understand This** - October 23, 2001 (Koch Records)
- **RetroActive** - June 23, 2009 (Babygrande Records)
- **The Contemporary Classics** - September 15, 2009 (Babygrande)
- **Black From The Future** - April 15, 2016 (Babygrande Records)

Music Videos

Brand Nubian

- "Slow Down"
  "Feels So Good"
  "All For One"
  "Love Me Or Leave Me Alone"
  "Punks Jump Up To Get Beat Down"

- "Allah U Akbar"
  "Word Is Bond"
  "Hold On"
  "Don't Let It Go Straight To Your Head"

Sadat X

- Notorious B.I.G. featuring Sadat X "Come On"
  "The Lump Lump"
  "Hang 'em High"
  Sadat X featuring Pete Rock - "Turn It Up"

- "Fake Out"
  "Stages and Lights"
  "I Know This Game"
  "We In New York"
  "Get Yours" featuring Black Rob
  "What Up Kid"
  Sadat X featuring Cormega and Lanelle Tyler - "On Fire"
  Sadat X featuring A-F-R-O & Rahzel The Legend "Murder Soundtrack"
  Sadat X featuring R.A. The Rugged Man & Thirstin Howl III "Industry Outcasts"
-

Lord Jamar

- "The Corner, The Streets/Original Man"

Grand Puba

- "360 (What Goes Around)"
"I Like It"
"A Little of This"
Grand Puba featuring Kid Capri, Lord Jamar & Sadat X "This Joint Right Here"
Mary J. Blige with Grand Puba - "What's The 411?" (Yo! MYV Raps 1993)
Grand Puba featuring Mary J. Blige - "Check It Out" (Remix)
Fat Joe featuring Grand Puba & Diamond D - "Watch The Sound"
Strickly Roots featuring Fat Joe & Grand Puba - "Beg No Friends"
MoKenStef featuring Grand Puba - "He's Mine" (Remix)
Grand Puba "UDK"

CHAPTER 3

Pete Rock & C.L. Smooth

Pete Rock & C.L. Smooth arrived on the scene in the midst of a Hip-Hop impasse of sorts. The music had officially crossed over to the mainstream. Classic artists and groups were running over themselves for a piece of the pie, and nothing was sacred.

Pete Rock was schooled in production by his cousin, DJ Eddie F. Eddie F is known for cultivating the talents of fellow Mount Vernon sons Heavy D, Al B. Sure, Dave "Jam" Hall, and even Diddy, who lived with him for a spell. Under the guise of Untouchables Entertainment, which is known as the first modern "production camp." F and D the cause "Money Earnin'" precedes Mount Vernon in Hip-Hop vernacular.

The dynamic duo of Pete Rock & C.L. Smooth met in High School after C.L. Smooth moved to New Rochelle from Hollis, Queens. Pete Rock was working with other emcees at the time, but when he first heard C.L. rhyme over a beat, he knew they had to work together. Climbing his way up the ladder one step at a time, Pete Rock had cultivated and created beats as an Untouchable managed by Eddie F for a who's who of Hip-Hop heavyweights. Together they formed the formidable duo known as Pete Rock & C.L. Smooth and set to work on breaking barriers artfully crafting a unique sound of their own that was brand new for the 90s. Fifty demo songs later they entered into a contract with Elektra Records.

When the **All Souled Out EP** arrived on Elektra Records June 25, 1991, the obscure smooth jazz and soul of Pete Rock coupled with the socially conscious and aware raps of C.L. Smooth created a groundswell of activity and infatuation of the duo. When Elektra released the classic long player Mecca and the Soul Brother on June 9, 1992, life was never the same.

Mecca and the Soul Brother is a first-hand rare opportunity to look directly into the mind, body and soul of its creators. Eighteen cuts, including interludes, its songs speak individually and possess character, a different emotion and those Pete Rock beats. Obligated to reach out to his brothers and sisters in need, C.L. Smooth's lyrical work is a shining example of a confident young man striving to enlighten and bring up his people.

Above all, Pete Rock & C.L. Smooth expressed their deep love of Hip-Hop and a steadfast desire to change it back to its core beginning of cuts, rhymes and a beat.

In The Beginning

You produce a lot of artists.

Pete Rock:
I do. I did such groups as Public Enemy, Slick Rick, Shabba Ranks, Chubb Rock, Father MC, EPMD, Heavy D, A Tribe Called Quest, Main Source.

Everybody.

Pete Rock:
Everybody. A lot of people.

How did you get into production?

Pete Rock:
It all comes from DJing. I've been Djing since I was seven just musically inclined. It just comes from DJing, and you want to reach to other levels, so I started producing with Eddie F. He taught me how to use the SP1200, the S900, and from then things just got bigger and better.

What does C.L. stand for?

C.L. Smooth:
C.L. stand for Corey Love, which was a street name that was given to me by my friends, by the people I've been dealing with and that just carried into the music business as a basic title.

The Process

J. Alexander Ferron: What comes first? The lyrics or the beats?

C.L. Smooth:
The track. The way I work it, the way that we worked it up 'till now, I'm always presented with any track I want. Any track that's made I go just in, and we pick together what's best for the group. It's a group thing. It's not too many people that are involved in our music. The capabilities we keep it between ourselves unless we're doing other people's production.

Mecca and the Soul Brother is a lengthy album. You are probably the first group to put out an album this long.

C.L. Smooth:
You get an album that has 18 cuts but it's not 18 songs, it's 18 cuts. You have interludes and stuff, but when you go out, and you buy an album, and you want a lot out of it, you want a little extra. There's nothing wrong with giving people extra as long as it's moving to the next level instead of just staying on a flat boundary and keep it at that. Just us going into the studio every day we make something better every time.

J. Alexander Ferron: How do you decide who gets what? Sometimes it seems like you give the best beats to other people.

Pete Rock:

The only reason why I don't is 'cause every beat I do it has to be fat. It got to be dope 'cause I don't want to look bad on the production tip, so that's basically how that goes. As far as me and C.L. Smooth go, we take a lot of concentration into doing what we're doing when we starting our new album, or when we doing something together. It's got to be dope. Pete Rock & C.L. Smooth are brand new for the 90's. This album that's coming out, double album that's coming out, the next album that we do has to be totally different from that. That's what a lot of brothers don't understand. They put out an album then they do the same shit over again. The same music, the same kind - They talk about the same topics, but ours is gonna be totally different every time. We gonna hit 'em.

C.L. Smooth:

We want each song to have its character. Each song to individually speak for themselves. When that particular song cuts off, that's the end of that. We going on to something else. And you have a full 18 cuts of different things, different emotions, different beats. I heard a guy say that "Well ... It doesn't - It's really - Your album is one tempo". I tend to disagree. I tend to think that it goes up and down and we've studied that. When we go in there, and we do our thing we study how long, how many bars there are and what is the tempo of the song. That's part of us going in and taking care of our business 100%. Instead of just going in and making a jam.

J. Alexander Ferron: A lot of the production is more complicated than what you usually find.

C.L. Smooth:

The reason why I can flow so well with it is because I know the speed of it. I know what it entails, and then when he makes it a lot of times he comes to me, and he tells me "Yo! C.L., when I made this beat, this is what I thought, this is what I thought immediately when I was making it." So that has a big difference in what storyline I use. If I use a storyline or if I'm talking about myself. Now, a lot of times I'm not perfect so I go in, and I do put some material on the wrong track, which doesn't have the depth enough to compare with the track, to blend in and coagulate. So it takes a lot of time for me to study the track and go in there and take care of business.

The Message

J. Alexander Ferron: What is your philosophy towards Rap?

C.L. Smooth:
It's a very large speaking situation where you have young brothers who have the capability to speak to a large amount of people and when you do that it's best that you say something positive nine times out of the ten. When you have that chance to speak to people, I feel it's an obligation for my group personally, to at least write one song where you're saying something positive towards the brothers and sisters who are not in a positive mind state or a positive area. To enlighten them on the things that are going on today.

On the beginning of the album, you explain what Mecca is. You say it's not part of the body; it's not part of the mind.

C.L. Smooth:
It's a way of life. You can judge a person by what they wear and where they stay, but that doesn't mean you know that person. That doesn't mean you know totally what that person is about, and what he manifests, and what he pertains to be, or what he could be. It just means that you are aware of where a person is in the physical but the way of life is just dealing with everyday problems and conquering them, and that's what Mecca is all about. Mecca is - It gives you the state of mind to understand the music, as well as what's being talked about in the song.

What did you grow up reading that got you into this frame of mind?

C.L. Smooth:
It took a particular book, **Message to the Black Man** by Elijah Mohamed, to enlighten me on just the word Mecca and to get me more into learning about what Mecca is all about, and what Mecca is to me and my partner. **Mecca and the Soul Brother**; what do they have in common? What makes it so special? The reason why we created **Mecca and the Soul Brother** is because like I told you before, you see a person in a certain place, and you know the name, but you don't know the outs, the inside of a person. So Mecca gave you an opportunity, a rare opportunity to learn the inside of Pete Rock & C.L. Smooth, rather than just the outside. Knowing who the group is and going to see them perform but you learn a little bit more, they give you a little bit more depth.

Ghost

J. Alexander Ferron: What's the story? Is it hectic or do you like to work?

C.L. Smooth:
I feel happy doing it because basically, I don't have to run out and jump down people's backs to get my tracks and to get my lyrics. It's from us. We go out, and we shop for our beats, and we think of our lyrics. There was only one particular time that early in our careers where we chose somebody to write for us. But that was only to balance out the level of my writing to establish myself and to get a different side of the switch, which happened on "The Creator", to get a different vibe, and it worked out rather well, and on the remix, we wrote new lyrics. So it helps us a lot. I would never tell a person you're less of a lyricist for having somebody write for you because I've gotten in there and I've written lyrics for a few people, and they couldn't get it. They couldn't get it down pat.

Who?

C.L. Smooth:
I'd rather not say but they just couldn't get down to it. It really takes a professional to get in there and write lyrics and also say lyrics. Writing them down is one thing. Saying 'em and expressing 'em and getting a particular thought out and getting the particular mood out is a totally different thing than writing. I have a brother. He can write. He can write well. He can write songs but he can't rap. You see what I'm saying? So when you have a different situation you like to ...

There's a lot you have to measure in order to have a successful group. There's a lot of things that you might have to sacrifice in the beginning. I didn't think I was any less of a writer because I let somebody else write on my album but I felt it was beneficial to let people know. "Well, okay, judge it from here. I seen another guy write for him and I'm listening to C.L.'s rap." Now, I didn't hear any comments that … "Well, C.L. shouldn't write anymore. He should have everybody write for him", or something like that. I always got complimented on whatever I did. I always made the right decision.

J. Alexander Ferron: The reason I got into Rap as a journalist was that I used to write raps but I could never say it, so it was frustrating.

C.L. Smooth:
But it offends a lot of people when you write their lyrics, and I'm learning that more and more every time, but I felt that being that we're a new group and being that we're confident enough and we've proven that not only can the writing … It's just not just one thing just not the writing. We could take our production and take somebody else's writing, and it'd still be us, and we bring it to the next level. So it can be either or. It can be the writing, or we both just put in enough time and work to get a credible song people will listen to.

That's what I get when listening to the album. You know what they're talking about. You would instead not write a song about a topic that you don't know about. You write about what you know about, and you really believe in it, and that's why it flows. That's why it sounds good and makes sense.

C.L. Smooth:

Yeah. Well, you have to be comfortable. I'm comfortable to a certain point, but it seems like when under pressure I'm a little bit more on point than I would be if I was just – if everything was just done for me. A lot of pressure has got me to this point. I mean, pressure is bad, but it's gotten me to the level where I want to be. It's trained me and conditioned me.

Nobody Beats The Biz

Uncredited sampling ran rampant through the Golden Age of Hip-Hop. Until Biz Markie, his label Cold Chillin' and its distributor Warner Bros. Records was served with a lawsuit by Gilbert O' Sullivan. O' Sullivan claimed his #1 song on the Billboard Top 100 chart "Alone Again (Naturally)" was featured as an unauthorised sample on the song "Alone Again" off the *I Need A Haircut* album. O'Sullivan won the case on December 17, 1991, in the United States District Court for the Southern District of New York and the Judge even referred the matter for Criminal Prosecution. Going forward samples had to be cleared by copyright owners with mechanical rights often making the practice cost prohibitive. The age of interpolation followed.

J. Alexander Ferron: Does the Biz Markie sampling case and decision affect you?

C.L. Smooth:
It affects us at the point where we have to realise that we're taking old music and we're reviving it, but there's the proper channels that you have to go through in order to use the production that we use. Now, Biz Markie isn't; he's not really in the place that we are. We have far greater capabilities and production than he does. He hasn't produced that many acts, so really, I don't know. I don't see his problem.

As a Producer are you going to enter the studio thinking different after Biz Markie?

Pete Rock:

Basically what happened just these people want to try to set an example that if you don't give us credit, we'll do this. We're careful. People get what they supposed to get when we sample our music. They'll get what they're supposed to; they'll get their credit. That's it.

Future

Do you think there is a place for C.L. Smooth and Pete Rock because what you're doing doesn't fit in with what's going on?

C.L. Smooth:
Well, what we're trying to do is change it back to cuts, rhyme and a beat. Put it back to the beginning where it all started. Not this dancing bullshit. Not people going into the studio and it's not them or shit like that. It's uncalled for. We don't believe in that. We believe if you have talent you have talent. I run into a lot of people that have a vast amount of talent that lives down the block from me, and here you have somebody who has a record deal and doesn't appreciate it. To go in there and they don't have the attitude that I know that a true person who has talent and would love to be in their place is not given a chance.

J. Alexander Ferron: What happened to Big Daddy Kane? The guy was amazing, and now he's putting out all this bullshit like ***Prince of Darkness***.

C.L. Smooth:
Well, I feel that his lyrical ability is still there. It's just he's picking the wrong tracks. Like I said before, you could put lyrics on anything.

That doesn't mean that it's gonna match the production, and what he's doing is not matching the production. His lyrical skills are far greater than his production. If he was to get with somebody who can match the production with his lyrical ability, no question he would be accepted again.

Is Gangster Rap hurting Rap?

C.L. Smooth:
No. But, I mean, I look at it like this though; somebody has to do it. Somebody is gonna come out with something that it just has curses in it. Guys are soldiers, man, and they're speaking about - They're going through a rough time right now, and they're laying it down on the tracks. So I can accept it as that, but I can't accept that as the total truth. I accept it as something that's going on. I accept it as something that is not part of my life right now because I'm doing something different. Either I can be ... Either or; I can be a gangster, or I can be an entertainer. You can be one or the other, but you can't be both.

Next

Shortly after the featured interview, on one cold New York City night in 1992, Pete Rock made history inside The Hit Factory Times Square using three separate rooms to record and remix three classic tracks.

Pete Rock & C.L. Smooth released **The Main Ingredient** on November 8, 1994. It was overlooked at the time but has grown into an essential piece of work owing to the natural evolution of the duo's sound and lyrics. Its three singles, "I Got A Love", "Take You There" and "Searching" continue to get play to this day. However, shortly after the release of "Searching" and a hot appearance in a Sprite commercial, they split up citing the ever-popular creative differences and a precarious working relationship. Pete Rock instantly levitated into the studio and stayed producing and remixing an endless stream of songs.

Pete Rock & C.L. Smooth regrouped in 1998 to record "Da Two" for Pete Rock's **Soul Survivor** album, and then again in 2001 for the Second edition of **PeteStrumentals** with "Back On The Block", and "It's A Love Thing" in 2004 for Soul Survivor II.

C.L. Smooth picked up the torch and recorded two solo albums, **American Me** in 2006 and **The Outsider** in 2007. Traffic Entertainment Group released the deluxe edition of **Mecca and the Soul Brother** on September 14, 2010. The package came replete with remixes, instrumentals, acappellas, poster and liner notes.

The package came replete with remixes, instrumentals, acappellas, poster and liner notes. Consequent to the untimely passing of GURU, the dynamic duo officially reunited putting their differences behind them and toured.

Pete Rock is responsible for over 25 million albums sold throughout his storied career producing artists from Notorious B.I.G. to Mick Jagger (unreleased), Madonna (unreleased) and Lady Gaga. In 2012, he won a Grammy for Rap Album of the Year for his contributions to Kanye West's **My Beautiful Dark Twisted Fantasy** on "Runaway" and bonus track "The Joy". He remains in demand creating beats and tours the world as a DJ.

C.L. Smooth has been in and out of the studio creating solid music under the radar. His long-awaited album **The Emancipation of Corey Penn** has been in the mix for over five years and is finally set to see the light of day, or is it?

Album Discography

Pete Rock & C.L. Smooth

- **All Souled Out** - June 25, 1991 (Elektra)
- **Mecca And The Soul Brother** - June 9, 1992 (Elektra)
- **The Main Ingredient** - November 8, 1994 (Elektra)
- **The Basement Demos EP** - February 17, 2009 (One Leg Up Records)

Pete Rock

- **Soul Survivor** - November 10, 1998 (Loud/RCA)
- **PeteStrumentals** - May 1, 2001 (BBE/Rapster)
- **Lost & Found: Hip Hop Underground Classics** - November 4, 2003 (BBE)
- **Soul Survivor II** - May 11, 2004 (BBE/Rapster)
- **My Own Worst Enemy with Ed O.G.** - November 9, 2004 (Fat Beats)
- **The Surviving Elements: From Soul Survivor II Sessions** - January 25, 2005 (BBE/Rapster)
- **Underground Classics** - September 19, 2006 (Rapster)

- **NY's Finest** - February 28, 2008 (Nature Sounds)
- **Monumental with Smif-N-Wessun** - June 28, 2011 (Duck Down)
- **PeteStrumentals 2** - June 23, 2015 (Mello Music)

C.L. Smooth

- **American Me** - October 31, 2006 (Shaman Work Recordings)
- **The Outsider** - August 21, 2007 (Blackheart Entertainment)
- **Multi Barz of Fury EP** - January 22, 2008 (St. Nick)
- **Man on Fire** with J Period **The Freestyle Sessions** (St. Nick)

Music Videos

Pete Rock & C.L. Smooth

- "They Reminisce Over You (T.R.O.Y.)"
- (Live on The Arsenio Hall Show) - "They Reminisce Over You (T.R.O.Y.)"
- "The Creator"
- "Straighten It Out"
- "Lots Of Lovin'"
- "I'll Take You There"
- "It's Not A Game"
- "I Got A Love"

Pete Rock

- Cosmic Slop
- Edo. G (Prod. by Pete Rock) - Make Music
- Pete Rock & Smif N Wessun - "Roses" feat. Freeway
- Pete Rock ft. Loose Ends - Take Your Time
- Sadat X Turn It Up feat. Pete Roc
- Pete Rock & Smif N Wessun - "Monumental" feat. Tyler Woods
- Verbal Kent "TAKE" produced by PETE ROCK
- Pete Rock - Till I Retire / Best Believe
- Pete Rock & Smif N Wessun - "Night Time" feat. Buckshot
- NOTTZ x PETE ROCK - Turn It Up

- Kurupt-Yessir (Prod By Pete Rock)
- Pete Rock & Smif N Wessun - "That's Hard" feat. Sean Price & Styles P
- Diamond D - Only Way 2 Go ft. Pete Rock
- InI Feat. Pete Rock - Fakin' Jax
- Pete Rock Featuring Kurupt & Inspectah Deck - Tru Master

C.L. Smooth

- "Anything for You"
- "Smoke In The Air"

Who Is Harris Rosen?

Father. Son. Brother.

Harris Rosen is the author of **NWA: The Aftermath**, **The Real Eminem: Broke City Trash Rapper**, and other Behind The Music Tales books. For twenty years, he self-published the national lifestyle magazine Peace! He lives in Toronto, Canada, with his son, Louis.

Rosen has interviewed hundreds of composers, artists, actors, and athletes. Including the Notorious B.I.G., Dr Dre, Daft Punk, Eminem, Derek Jeter, Georges St. Pierre, Nirvana, Metallica, Chris Rock, Buju Banton, Beastie Boys, Kiss, Destiny's Child and Aaliyah to list a few.

He has gone to six continents and was in the midst of a whirlwind of multiple musical, cultural revolutions that occurred throughout the 90's and 2000s while compiling a genuine and honest archive of audio, images and video.

behindthemusisctales.com

facebook -/behindthemusictales/

instagram - harrisrosenbtmt

twitter - @mrheller1

Urgent Plea

Thank you for reading my book.

I appreciate all of your comments, and I love hearing what you have to say.

I need your input to make the next book in this series better. Please leave a helpful review wherever you got this copy letting me know what you thought of this book.

Thanks so much!!

OTHER BOOKS BY HARRIS ROSEN

N.W.A: The Aftermath

The Real Eminem Broke City Trash Rapper

The Real Destiny's Child: The Writing's On The Wall

New York State of Mind 1.0

The Reasonings of Buju Banton, Bounty Killer & Sizzla

Magnolia Home of tha Soliders: Behind the Scenes with the Cash Money Millionaires

The Real 213

The Real MC Eiht: Geah

The Real Diddy

The Real Daft Punk

BEHINDTHEMUSICTALES.COM